Rebirth Into Pure Land

Other books by Robert (Bob) Sachs:

The Complete Guide to Nine Star Ki
Health for Life

Rebirth Into Pure Land

*A True Story of Birth, Death
and Transformation*

by Robert Sachs

published by
Zivah Publishers

© Bob Sachs 1993

Published by
Zivah Publishers
P.O. Box 13192
Albuquerque, NM 87192-3192

Book Designed and Edited by
Margaret A. Thompson

Cover Designed by
Lisa Graff

Printed by
Gilliland Printing, Inc.
Arkansas City, KS

The book was set in Book Antiqua
and Ribbon 131 Bd BT

ISBN 0-9622707-9-2

First Printing, October 1994

13 12 11 10 9 8 7 6 5 4 3 2

TABLE OF CONTENTS

FOREWORD 7

AUTHOR'S NOTES 8

THE HRI 9

A SPECIAL DEDICATION TO PARENTS WHO HAVE LIVED

THROUGH SIDS 11

THE MEANINGS OF PURE LAND 15

REASONS 17

PREPARATION 21

THE VISIT 27

THE BIRTH 33

FORTY-EIGHT DAYS 39

OLE COMES TO VISIT 43

DEATH AND REBIRTH 51

TEN DAYS OF MIRACLES 65

TEN YEARS LATER 83

AUSPICIOUS COINCIDENCES 89

A LETTER AND EPILOGUE FROM MIDWIFE NONI RHODES   95

GLOSSARY 97

USEFUL ADDRESSES 103

"In language that is clear and faith that is expressed both in depth and simplicity, Robert Sachs tells of his family's response to the SIDS death of their infant daughter, Shamara. Seen through the heart of his Buddhist faith, it is a journey with meaning for everyone burdened with technological limitations and searching for spiritual meaning in life and death."

Carrie Sheehan
Former Senior Consultant,
SIDS Alliance

"*Rebirth Into Pure Land* helps us appreciate that all tragedies bring with them an opportunity for growth and under-standing. Being a SIDS parent myself, I can unequivocally state that the little ones that we lost continue to touch and influence all the lives of those who loved them."

Kari E. Brandenburg
NM Chapter,
SIDS Alliance

"As a practicing psychotherapist and marriage, family and child therapist I highly recommend Robert Sachs' book as an inspiring and *therapeutic* vehicle for healing the wounds of grief and loss as well as showing us the benefits and support of strong spiritual practice and loving community."

Loic Jassy Ph.D., Psychotherapist
Los Gatos and Soquel, CA

FOREWORD

In the mystery of life and of death, there are more alternatives than imagination can conjure. This is the remarkable story of the grace that is our own great deathless nature and the grief, too, that even heaven cannot wholly eradicate.

This is a book of options, an honoring of the continuum that few have believed possible. It is a rare tale about the death of a child and the rebirth of the spirit in the hearts of all who were near - and the skillful passing into what is available to us all - our original nature.

Stephen Levine
Author of *Who Dies?*

AUTHOR'S NOTES

Rebirth Into Pure Land takes place within the context of Buddhist spiritual practice and in the lives of two westerners, myself, Bob Sachs, and my wife, Melanie Sachs, who are trying to integrate the Buddhist way of living and being in the world into our contemporary Western lives.

Because the events occurred within the context of such practice and philosophy, it seems important to include some of the Sanskrit and Tibetan words associated with the practice. I feel that the story itself is so powerful that the use of such terminology will not weaken its impact. And, for the curious, I have created a glossary. Anyone who wants to learn more about the words - how they are pronounced and what they mean - can do so.

It is my hope that this story will inspire all who come into contact with it.

Several people have helped to technically bring this book into being. Thanks go to Nancy Reinstein for typing, Susan Biggs for editorial comments, Lisa Graff for her cover design and Margaret Thompson, my editor and publisher. Thanks also go to Lisa Hanaway and to Sidney Piburn of Snow Lion Publications for their encouragement, and of course, my wife and partner, Melanie who has been there throughout, helped in every aspect and lovingly reminded me when memory failed.

THE HRI

Hri is a sound of unconditional universal compassion.

Hri is a sound that ensures that compassion is used wisely.

Hri is a symbol for Dewachen, the Western Pure Land.

A SPECIAL DEDICATION TO PARENTS WHO HAVE LIVED THROUGH SIDS

Shamara Phillipa, our daughter, died of what was clinically labeled "Sudden Infant Death Syndrome" or SIDS. This is perhaps the most incomprehensible of deaths a parent - or for that matter, anyone - can face. What causes a baby who seems to be perfectly healthy to just stop breathing and die? While medical science searches for its answer to that question, babies continue to die and families continue to be devastated. Parents are left with their feelings of anxiety, guilt, frustration, anger and depression. Overwhelmed with these feelings, they go through varying levels of physical and mental debilitation. I have been told that statistically, parents who have endured the agony of SIDS often end up parting ways.

As you read this account of Shamara Phillipa's short life with us, you will learn how our spiritual perspectives and practices provided us with a wellspring of strength from which to draw in order to pass through all the physical and emotional pain. It seems to me that any parent who undergoes the ordeal of SIDS, regardless of the spiritual path he or she has chosen to honor, will, by nature, experience such feelings in dealing with the loss of a child. However, the degree to which we know and love ourselves and the amount of work we have done in developing a view of life which can embrace even this tragedy will determine how well we handle our circumstances and whether or not we will, once again, be able to affirm life.

❖ ❖ ❖

Having said all this, there are a few general words we want to offer to each of you. Although this story is couched in Buddhist terminology and concepts, how we went through and integrated this experience into our lives can easily be taken to heart by anyone, regardless of religious or spiritual orientation.

Please know that your child came into and passed out of this world for some good purpose. Perhaps it was for the child; perhaps for you. Strive to seek meaning in your child's little life, rather than becoming trapped in the pain of your loss.

As parents we do the best we can with what we know. Trust that you offered your best to this little spirit and that it left for its own reasons, not because of anything you did. Life is a schoolhouse. Unless we are already saints, we are learning as we go. Be accepting of your own pain and whatever feelings arise. And don't expect or have the expectation laid upon you that by such and such a time or date that you should be "over it." Love yourself and allow healing to come in its own organic way.

If you are a part of a couple, make every effort to stay together. There are two things that often drive couples apart: blaming each other and the fear that if they get pregnant again, that SIDS will happen again. Don't let blame and fear rule your lives. You came together in love. In rekindling that love, you can find peace and comfort. Now more than ever you can discover the unconditional love and understanding that is the deeper reason you chose each other in the first place. It is time to open yourself. Be willing to be vulnerable with each other.

By opening yourself up at a time when closing down seems infinitely easier, there is the possibility of discovering that before, during and after this event, divine forces have been trying to tell you something about life itself. Don't shy away from the message of the divine. There are miracles constantly happening in the ordinariness of life. And sometimes these miracles show us that what we have thought of as being the ordinary, physical world has been limited by perceptions and ideas that until this time have never been challenged. A shift of perception may lead to your discovery of potential within yourself you may barely have glimpsed or have been too timid to express.

Lastly, seek out others who are attempting to open their hearts and minds. Perhaps you will find them in a SIDS group; perhaps in a religious or spiritual community. Such people may even just manifest in your life as you are opening and changing. In any event, never forget that although we come into and go out of this world alone, that while we are here, there is no need to be lonely.

You are loved. Beyond all others mentioned in this story of *Rebirth Into Pure Land*, this book is dedicated to you. May it serve in your healing and growth.

Bob and Melanie

THE MEANINGS OF PURE LAND

The title of this book, *Rebirth Into Pure Land*, has two meanings.

It literally has to do with the death of our daughter, Shamara, and her subsequent rebirth into the Western Pure Land of the Amitabha Buddha - as confirmed by Phowa Master Ole Nydahl and my root teacher, the Venerable Khenpo Karthar Rinpoche.

It is also about how these events revealed to us a sacred vision of reality. This vision has become the wellspring from which Melanie and I have continued to practice and commit ourselves to the teachings of the Buddha and have striven to integrate these teachings into every aspect of our being through our thoughts, words, actions and accomplishments. Our purpose and joy in life is to help others in any way we can to see this vision as well.

CHAPTER ONE

REASONS

I have many reasons for wanting to write this factual account of the events of and around the birth, death and transference of consciousness of our baby daughter, Shamara Phillipa.

Shamara would have been 10 years old on December 1, 1993. Ironically, I find myself beginning this true story of her life 4 months before her birth, in August of 1983 - exactly 10 years to the month prior to when I became inspired to write her story.

For, soon after her death and transference, then later in times of quiet reflection, glimpses and recognition of the forces at work even before her birth came to both my wife, Melanie, and me. So much of what took place in the few months before Shamara's birth, in the 48 days that she was alive with us and in her passing has influenced the course and direction of our lives since. Thus, first and foremost, this short account is a testimony and a gesture of appreciation to Shamara for what she brought to us.

Shamara's two sisters, Kai Ling and Christina, also live with the memory of Shamara in their hearts. No two little girls could have been prouder of a little sister than they were. On the day that Shamara left her body, a small bright light went out of Kai's and Tina's eyes. Children cannot rationalize away death as we adults often do. Witnessing death at such tender ages of five and three has no doubt left an almost incomprehensible, yet powerful message in their minds about the fragility and tenuousness of life.

Even though the tears have been shed and the years have passed, Shamara's memory still shows itself in Kai's and Tina's loving regard and care for those around them. Melanie and I see and hear it in their expression of hopes, fears and dreams for their own lives. This book is also written in the hope of dispelling any pain, suffering or confusion that they may still be burdened with and of being able to share with them the deepened appreciation for the ebb and flow of life that Melanie and I have arrived at as a result of Shamara's sojourn through our lives.

I have also written this account as an acknowledgement of the remarkable people who played a part in these events; friends, teachers, even strangers, who stepped forward without hesitation to help, support and play their part in the events and miracles of those times. As I document events and moments in the lives of others who shared in them, my hope is to bring people together, particularly those of my Kagyu family who, I feel, find themselves caught up in what disguises itself as a holy war. Through telling this story, it is my hope that friends will once again be reminded of why we all came to Lord Buddha's teachings in the first place.

CHAPTER TWO

PREPARATION

$\mathcal{I}$n mid-August of 1983 I returned home to Lexington, Kentucky after spending some precious time with my spiritual teacher, the Venerable Khenpo Karthar Rinpoche, in Woodstock, New York and in Boston with the man who, through the years, has taught me how to eat and live from day to day, Michio Kushi. From Michio I was able to bring back a great deal of useful information for the physician whose holistic health clinic I worked in. From Khenpo Rinpoche, I returned with practical ways to dissolve illusion as well as a promise from him to come to teach in Lexington in the late fall.

I had driven the 17 hours straight from upstate New York to be with Melanie, the inspiration in my life, and our two daughters, Kai and Tina. I was both exhausted and elated. In the days that followed, Melanie and I would sort out all the pieces of the trip. With the news that Khenpo Rinpoche wanted to visit Lexington there was suddenly a lot more to do.

In fact, there was a lot to do anyway. There was getting back to work and being on a schedule. There was the daily running of the house, the garden and two very busy little girls. Kai was about to enter kindergarten and Tina, a Montessori pre-school. And Melanie was 5 months pregnant.

We normally found ourselves busy, dealing with our immediate family and home life and a circle of friends with whom we connect wherever we live - people who want to share in the knowledge we have made a point of gathering for the sole purpose of passing on to others.

However, what we were engaged in at that moment had a deeply intense quality about it. Both of us were keenly aware of the responsibility of bringing Khenpo Rinpoche to a new city to teach and we were trying to prepare ourselves for a higher level of public responsibility and involvement.

In addition, Melanie's pregnancy, which occurred simultaneously to these events, made us quite introspective. Perhaps our state of introspection was because the conception of the child had come about as a part of a process of healing some old wounds which had kept Melanie and me estranged for a time. But there seemed to be more to it. The constant motion of our lives and demands on our time made it difficult to pinpoint exactly what it was we were feeling. Still, we felt like we were moving through something together. On the one hand, it was reassuring. On the other, each day presented us with an uncertainty that we had not experienced before.

During the week, I was at work with my friends at the Holistic Medical Center. I was writing out the material from my Boston visit with Michio Kushi and seeing clients one after another. I spent my evenings and weekends building a shrine room in the attic space of our house in preparation for Khenpo Rinpoche's visit. Melanie, meanwhile, was busy getting our daughters off to school, tending the garden and preparing the house for Rinpoche's visit and the expected early winter arrival of our newest family member. In her "spare" time she was teaching cooking classes and organizing publicity schedules of volunteers for Khenpo Rinpoche's visit. In these months, we spoke at meals, talked over details on the phone and saw each other only briefly before exhaustion overcame us at night. Not much time to reflect - just do.

Doing what we do, being how we are, we certainly had the community buzzing! We have always enjoyed creating meaningful events for friends wherever we live. And in Lexington, we were involved in the Tibetan Buddhist community, holding large gatherings at Tibetan New Year and hosting our dear Dharma brother and sister, Ole and Hannah Nydahl, in their whirlwind teaching circuits across America.

Ole had come to visit us every year since we met him in Woodstock during His Holiness Karmapa's last tour to America in 1980. He has an almost contagious energy which inspires enthusiasm for healthy spiritual practice and has often been the front runner and ground breaker for the great Tibetan teachers to come to new locations where welcoming and like-minded friends are eager to connect with their true nature.

And now, our own teacher, the spiritual grandfather of our children, was coming to Lexington. The community's sense of wonder, appreciation and desire to be part of this local, historic event was both touching and inspiring.

Peter Blunt prepared a wooden platform for a throne. Ed Baker came by to help tape the sheet rock in the shrine room. Dick Levine and Anne Frye, who to this day keep Khenpo Rinpoche's teachings alive in Lexington, arranged for him to teach at the University of Kentucky.

Other friends volunteered to work and clean during the visit; Laurel Thatcher, Mara Genthner, Adelle Prager, Mrs. Govinda Rajalu, to name a few. There were our "guardian angels," Geoff and Diana Bullington, who arranged for a public talk. Geoff and Di have always been in the background for us. That's where they like to be. They were the first couple I met when I was invited by physician and friend Walt Stoll, to come to the Holistic Medical Center in Lexington to teach foot reflexology. Geoff and Di used their truck to help us with the move to Lexington from Columbus. We lived with them while we looked around for a house in town. They have become our daughters' honorary aunt and uncle. Geoff and Di remain in our hearts as practical guides in the ways of spirit beyond any dogmatic allegiance to this or that school or tradition. And the connection that Melanie and I have with Geoff and Di was to become most apparent in the months that followed.

And then there was the pregnancy. We had always done home births for our children and saw no reason to make an exception this time. We were fortunate in that one of the best midwives in the region, Noni Rhodes, lived one street over. Our daughter, Kai, and Noni's daughter, Kelly, were the closest of friends. Melanie already spent much of her mom-to-mom, friend-to-friend time with Noni. Now she met with Noni and her partner, Debbie Neal, on a regular schedule.

And there was the support of my friend and colleague, Walt Stoll, a remarkable physician who has been a pioneer advocate of holistic and preventive health care. Walt is charismatic and sometimes a bit "overly direct" with clients, media or whomever he felt needed to hear what he had to say. His bluntness sometimes daunted Melanie. But in us, Walt could see a couple committed to health standards and ways of living that he both admired and aspired to. He did routine checks on Melanie throughout the pregnancy and, as a colleague and friend, was both honored and excited to attend Melanie's delivery - and be emergency backup if needed.

In addition to the professional support we had for the impending birth, many friends came forward in various helpful ways. The energy that Melanie and I had been giving to the community was being returned in kind by friends who eagerly awaited the arrival of our newest family member.

We were feeling, at once, caught up in our respective whirlwinds of activity and extremely blessed. The time was intense and action packed. There was a sense of joy and anticipation. And yet, somehow, in the background, both of us felt that these powerful and extraordinary events in our lives were moving us toward a time which had a deeper and as yet hidden message for us.

CHAPTER THREE

THE VISIT

One month almost to the day before Melanie's due date, Khenpo Rinpoche was on his way from Columbus, Ohio to Lexington.

Of course, the timing of preparation for his visit was down to the last minute. Final touches on the shrine room were done the night before. The gaps in the cooking, cleaning and interview schedules were filled in that day as well. With everything as organized as it can be before such a visit, there was the usual calm before the storm.

When a great spiritual master comes for a visit, there is a seemingly endless list of details which need attention. Our experience has taught us that the left brain or organizational mind seems to go on vacation once a master arrives. To avoid going crazy, we have learned to plan what we can with the full recognition that karmic unfoldment has its own timing and that the spiritual teacher is more attuned to that clock than to the one on the wall. One learns to plan and then let go.

In those moments before Rinpoche's arrival, there was an extraordinary mixture of qualities: clarity, anxiety and fuzzy-headedness from all the late nights. And, for Melanie, there were Braxton Hicks contractions - a type of contraction that some women get during the latter stages of pregnancy. Their frequency and intensity appeared to be proportional to the degree she found herself overdoing it.

In keeping with my own neurotic behavior, the thought of abandoning my incessant anticipatory pacing coincided with Rinpoche's arrival. And, in the first moments of seeing him, Melanie and I watched our attention to our daily lives give way to the single-minded purpose of serving Rinpoche and all those who awaited his presence in our community.

Since it was the first time he had visited this particular house of ours, we took Rinpoche and his translator (and our good friend), Ngodrup Burkhar, up to our attic to see the shrine room. Freshly painted in sky blue, it was as if the whole room opened to the heavens. Rinpoche liked it, especially the sloping ceilings which met the walls at a height of three feet and six inches. Sitting around the edge of the room, one had to remind oneself not to get up too quickly, lest one bang one's head on the ceiling. Rinpoche said that this was good as it helped people to stay mindful.

Upon seeing the shrine and the throne, he must have quickly developed some plans. For as soon as he was settled into his living quarters, Ngodrup approached me with a shopping list. In no time, he and I were doing what is so customary to a lama or Rinpoche's visit - shopping.

First on the list was to get a large, ornate frame for a

picture of His Holiness, the 16th Karmapa. Then we were off to a toy store to get gifts for our children and the children of friends who would visit. And we were also instructed to get some playdough. I did not know why playdough was such a priority but I soon learned of its great potential in Tantric ritual.

After Rinpoche settled in and the shopping was completed, the week passed in a magical way. Evening talks brought the interested and curious from around the state to Lexington. All of our friends from the local Dharmadhatu were there, as well as friends from the Zen and holistic health communities and others to whom we would grow closer over the remainder of our years in Lexington.

A weekend of meditation instruction and practice gave new students the opportunity to learn from a true master and old students the opportunity to experience deeper and richer dimensions to their practice and a greater appreciation for the Kagyu Lineage.

The movement in and through our house was continuous; friends were dropping off food, cleaning, having interviews with Rinpoche. It is in those times that one is functioning like the great saint, Chenrezig, with 1,000 arms and several sets of eyes. Amidst it all I would watch Melanie, going through contractions, handling the crowds, growing more radiant each day in the field of Rinpoche's kindness and the natural, magical glow that a woman emanates as the day of birthing approaches.

Melanie had done a brilliant job of arranging the house to suit Rinpoche's needs and the continuous daily traffic of events. She had decided that the only place she could not straighten up was the basement. And, in keeping with the way of such events, Khenpo Rinpoche spent much of his spare time in the basement cutting small pieces of wood for some unknown reason.

Other precious moments between events and resting would find him in a rocking chair in his room with one or the other of our daughters on his lap while he fed them grapes, cookies and candies. The love and care he has shown them over the years has given the purest teaching on who the Buddha is and what the Dharma offers. Even in their rebellious teen years, both Kai and Tina get excited with the prospect of seeing him.

Rarely is there time to reflect with people on their interviews during the visit but a few friends had remarkable experiences that they wanted to share. Our friend and birthing doctor, Walt, who has great clarity in seeing auras and energy fields, reported to us that in coming to and leaving his interview, he could see large beams of light radiating from our attic shrine room where Rinpoche sat.

Then there was a new friend, David Sawyer, a master of the *I Ching*, who, upon entering the shrine and before saying anything, was asked by Rinpoche through the translator to do an *I Ching* reading for Rinpoche's brother. David had never met Khenpo Rinpoche. The impact of Rinpoche's total clairvoyant awareness of David's skill was the initial fuel to inspire David to round up a contingent of his friends from Berea, Kentucky to help the monastery in Woodstock. To this day, he remains a diligent Dharma student committed to helping the Tibetan people. We honor him, his wife Jenny, friends Stan, Cameron, Ed, late-friend Janey and others in the hills of Kentucky who humbly practice and serve spirit in such gracious ways.

When one hosts a teacher, it is not uncommon to find that there is little private time with him to ask specific, personal questions. This indeed was the case in this visit. However, in hindsight, we realized that there was one aspect of our conversations with Rinpoche where there was a rather obvious omission.

We have seen Rinpoche before and since that visit around expectant mothers. We have always observed his excitement and seen how he has given blessings to them for the birth. In the midst of his kindness and spiritual energy, this omission in our interactions and conversations with him was not noted by either Melanie or me.

But Rinpoche obviously knew more than he was prepared to say - at least to us. For, as we later learned, in his interview with our two "guardian angels" Geoff and Diana, Rinpoche made what seemed to them a rather odd but urgent request. He asked them to take care of us over the next few months. This was said in confidence and we only learned of these remarks when it became clear to Geoff and Di what Rinpoche had seen with his pure vision but would only allude to in their interview.

Rinpoche left a permanent mark in the hearts of our friends and on the soul of Lexington, Kentucky. A Karma Kagyu Dharma study group was established in our attic at that time. He had demonstrated to us through his direct kindness, teaching and simple, yet skillful means how our minds can transform even the most mundane feelings, perceptions and objects into sources of pure inspiration. He had shown us a spiritual realm worth taking refuge in. Even playdough and wooden sticks became transformed into shrine offerings worth venerating. Indeed, our entire neighborhood had been transformed into a Pure Land.

And perhaps it is in the radiance of this perception that all of what was to transpire in the months to come took place.

CHAPTER FOUR

THE BIRTH

*I*t takes about one week to catch up on sleep and reorient oneself to everyday affairs after such visits. At the same time, the intensity of Rinpoche's visit seemed to blend into our preparation for Melanie's birthing. People who had made themselves available to us and were experiencing the blessing of Khenpo Rinpoche were now available to help out with these preparations. And the momentum and excitement around this imminent event began to infect everyone around us.

Our friends gave Melanie an elaborate baby shower - the magnitude of which we had not experienced before the birth of either Kai or Tina. What was most striking to Melanie about this event was how profoundly generous, almost to the point of extravagance, people were with their gift offerings. At first we thought that perhaps our friends were simply expressing their appreciation to us for bringing Khenpo Rinpoche and his teachings to them. However, Melanie's sense was that it was as if they were preparing to honor someone very special who was getting ready to enter their lives.

Beyond this "regal" shower, the support group of professionals who were to assist us before, during and after Melanie's labor and delivery was pulling together in a very powerful, focused and somewhat surprising manner. A macrobiotic acquaintance I had made in Boston during my visit with Michio Kushi appeared and offered himself as cook to help Melanie during and after labor. David was wild, but as a macrobiotic cook focusing on strengthening and healing, he was a genius. Midwives Noni and Debbie and even our physician, Walt, were expressing their excitement. The fact that a physician and two midwives were all willing to attend the birth and work together was a bit unusual in itself.

And yet, in the midst of all this activity, Melanie and I felt quite sober. We had gone through births before and had felt the full range of emotions that such events evoke. However, this time was different. We did not know exactly why it was different, but every fiber of our being was telling us to be quiet, to be open and to listen.

On December 1, 1983, Melanie woke up, fed the children and walked Kai to school. As she was returning home she felt unusually quiet. She wasn't sure just what was going on. She decided to go over to Noni's for a cup of tea and while there called me. She just wanted to chat and then go on home. Upon hearing her voice, my intuition told me to tell her to get checked by Noni. In fact, at this point, she was already through most of the first stages of labor.

When I arrived home, Melanie was already there and home birth preparations were in full swing. While we have had midwives and physicians either present or to back us up, I have always been the primary birth attendant; being with Melanie through all the stages of labor, giving her massages, letting her vent herself through whatever labor has taken her into. It is a sacred event where only truth resides and egos are not welcome.

What was so unusual about her labor this time was that Melanie was much quieter and much more focused than she had been in the past. If she was experiencing any discomfort at all, it seemed, from an observer's perspective, to be insignificant in light of whatever else she was going through internally as transition arrived.

By this time all the participants had arrived - except for one, of course. Walt was with us, along with Noni and Debbie. We had sent friends to retrieve Kai and Tina from school. And there was David, who prepared liquids and nourishment throughout.

Melanie's waters broke to low guttural sounds that she drew forth from deep within herself. She showed no signs of anguish, just an expression of deep concentration and the resolve to allow herself to be the portal through which our child would emerge to find a welcome home. It was not long from the time that Melanie entered transition that our daughter came silently into the world. And, as is customary for Melanie and me, the first sounds we spoke to her were the syllables of the mantra of Karmapa - *KARMAPA CHENO*.

Once the umbilical chord stopped pulsating, it was cut. Then the midwives bathed our daughter and lay her close to Melanie. Kai and Tina cuddled around their new sister. David stood by silently. Walt was moved to tears. Later he told us that in his 20 years experience as a physician he had never been to any birth like the one he had just witnessed. Melanie and I have always tried to make a sacred ritual of the births of our children. And this one was no exception. But beyond this, there was another quality present - something new, something serene - and perhaps that was what Walt was sensing.

Melanie and I never think of names for our children prior to their birth. It is our belief that, upon arrival, the child will let us know what it wishes to be called. It took about two hours for us to realize that our new daughter was to be called Shamara Phillipa Sachs.

Her middle name, Phillipa, was in memory of my favorite uncle who had recently passed away. Shamara was a derivation of the name of a high Tibetan teacher, His Eminence Shamar Rinpoche, with whom we had had the unique opportunity to spend time when he first came to Columbus, Ohio.

Our first encounter with Shamar Rinpoche was unique in the sense that it was both informal and personal. He came to the meditation center in Columbus soon after His Holiness Karmapa had visited. No one had met him and no one really knew who he was. Because of this, people had not prepared for his arrival and they asked Melanie and me if we would be available to let him into the center and make him feel comfortable. Few of the high teachers speak good English. He was one who did and it was remarkable to have a complete afternoon serving him and being able to talk to him about practice, our experiences with His Holiness the Karmapa and whatever else came to mind. What was most striking to me in our conversations was the feeling that I was continuing prior conversations and receiving further clarification on questions I had discussed with His Holiness. It was as though it was the same mind in a different body. To this day, His Eminence feels most like and reminds me of His Holiness.

In the days that followed, Shamar Rinpoche got to know our entire family. He commented on the unique qualities of our second daughter, Tina, and we told him that His Holiness had asked us to contact him in Sikkim upon her birth. He then sent her Dharma name to us through Ponlop Rinpoche. To this day she has a strong connection to the Dharma and a profound appreciation for practice.

As for my connection to Shamar Rinpoche, I had the unusual and auspicious opportunity to be given instruction on the nature of mind in the backyard of the center, alone with him. Such opportunities as this have always been rare and, with the increased demands upon and busier schedules of the Rinpoches and Eminences, are becoming even more so.

Perhaps that is why, two-and-one-half years later, without having seen or communicated with him through any conventional means, my mind turned to him as an inspiration when naming our daughter. In the hours that followed her birth, the significance of her name and the connection we had to Shamar Rinpoche became magically apparent.

Once Melanie had had a few hours in which to eat, get settled with Shamara and rest, we decided to call Karma Triyana Dharmachakra (KTD) in Woodstock so that we could inform Khenpo Rinpoche of her birth and request a Dharma name for her. It was late afternoon, so I knew that the KTD office was closed. Still, I had the office manager's home number. Pat Cliett was the manager in those days.

When I got Pat on the phone, I told him about the birth and asked if he could request from Rinpoche a name for Shamara. Although I cannot recall verbatim what he said next, the message was clear. "Well," he said, "I can get hold of Khenpo Rinpoche if you like. But Shamar Rinpoche has just unexpectedly arrived here. I could ask him."

It would have taken an act of extreme stupidity on my part to somehow not see such an obvious auspicious coincidence. Without hesitation, I asked Pat to please do this for us and Shamara. Roughly one week later, a Dharma card sent from His Eminence arrived with our daughter's name and His Eminence's Dharma seal. By then His Eminence had left Woodstock. However, I wanted to call Pat to thank him for his efforts on our behalf. Pat told us that the name given to Shamara was also - as I recall - His Eminence's sister's name; Karma Chime Donma; the Immortal Torch.

CHAPTER FIVE

FORTY-EIGHT DAYS

T he days that followed were quiet. Melanie and I do not invite many guests to our home during the first days when one of our children is getting used to being in the world. Melanie needed to rest and I stayed home to prepare meals and look after Kai and Tina.

Every morning when we awoke, these two little girls would scramble into our room to look at and fondle their new sister. There was such pride and joy in their faces when Melanie would allow one of them to hold Shamara. They obediently went to school each morning, but upon returning home it was obvious that their hearts and minds had been with Shamara the whole time.

Our friends could not constrain themselves forever and flowers and cards soon began to arrive. But only a few people actually came by. Partly it was because of the weather. But it also seemed that our usually busy house was cloaked in a shroud that let only a few close friends in. What we later learned was that those who did come had first impressions of Shamara that were very much in keeping with her demeanor. She was a quiet, pensive child. She didn't coo, chortle or cry very much as one would have expected from an infant. Of course, when she was hungry she cried, but not in a very insistent way. During her waking hours, she seemed content just to look around. She would fuss if she was held too long and seemed most content when simply left alone. Her worst time of day was just before bed. She seemed to have more difficulty settling down at that time of the early evening than either Kai or Tina had had at her age. Yet, rocking or nursing her brought little comfort and she usually drifted off more easily when we simply left her alone in her cot.

One friend remarked that when she came to visit, she somehow felt that treating Shamara as an infant was not appropriate. In fact, she said that in Shamara's presence she wanted to kneel in respect. It was an odd remark to make but Melanie and I completely understood her sentiment.

My interaction with Kai and Tina as tiny babies had been very different from my interaction with Shamara. I had held and talked to both of them quite a lot. The emotional bonds were very warm. I was their Dad and it felt good.

But with Shamara, I almost felt that such behavior was not what she was asking from me. When I held her, it was as though she wanted me to simply be silently present. Her eyes had a haunting quality about them. In the first few weeks, as a newborn baby takes in the world, any appearance of a direct visual focus on anyone or anything is simply accidental. Within a month, however, the baby's gaze generally becomes more direct and the contact more tangibly human. However, in the 48 days of Shamara's life we have no memories or photographs which would indicate that she ever made that shift in perception.

Probably the most meaningful contact I had with Shamara was within the context of meditation practice. I found myself reciting certain mantras to her: those of Chenrezig or the Bodhisattva of Compassion and of the Karmapa.

When I arose early in the morning she would stir. But, rather than demanding to be nursed, she was content for me to carry her into the shrine room where, often for the next hour and one half, she would gaze wide-eyed at our shrine. The noise of the bell and damaru which can be jarring to the senses when unfamiliar or unexpected never seemed to startle her. Being with Shamara in these times was like being with a close sangha member. When Shamara began to get distracted, often toward the end of practice, Melanie - who was most appreciative of the additional rest - would come to get her for her morning nursing and bath.

The Dharma teaches about precious human birth and about impermanence. It teaches that while we can have the perfect physical and environmental conditions for practice and spiritual transformation, that this opportunity is both rare and fragile as a bubble. Indeed, when tending to children, you are aware of their vulnerability and how much they need your love and care to keep them safe and ensure that their needs are met.

But, it is not necessarily a thought that crosses your mind that your baby will die. However, in our case, even though both our midwives and Walt reported to us how healthy and strong Shamara was at checkups, each morning we were amazed that she was actually still alive. And no matter how irrational and unlikely the thought and feelings seemed to us, it was impossible to rid ourselves of them.

The incident that stands out most as a reflection of our state of mind occurred at Christmas. Being English, Melanie has always enjoyed preparing a traditional English-style Christmas event; from tree to stockings, traditional songs to a mid-day Christmas dinner. All of us were feeling festive throughout the morning as stockings were emptied of their treats and presents were opened. However, this mood changed when it came time to prepare the dinner.

Dinner was traditionally roast turkey with stuffing, potatoes and the like. On Christmas morning, Melanie began to have and express anxiety about preparing the turkey. Finally she openly confessed that handling it felt like handling a dead child. It was so unbearable that she could not even walk into the kitchen where it was resting on the counter. Yet, because we had traditionally celebrated the day in this manner and did not want to disappoint the children, we tried to blank out the tormenting thoughts and carry on.

So, on that Christmas day, I prepared the turkey. Eating it later on felt almost sacrilegious.

CHAPTER SIX

OLE COMES TO VISIT

*I*t was on January 16, 1983, on the 47th day of Shamara's life that our good friend Ole Nydahl came for a visit.

I first met Ole in April of 1975 when he was driving the great Kagyu Yogi, Kalu Rinpoche, through Europe. I was taking a break from my counseling training and had gone back to Kagyu Samye Ling Tibetan Centre in Eskdalemuir, Scotland for a short retreat. What seemed odd to me at that time was that virtually everyone I had previously met at Samye Ling was there all at one time. Initially I thought that everyone had taken up residence and that I was the only one really returning for a visit; not exactly clear logic. Soon enough I found out that most of these friends had returned for the same reason - to see Kalu Rinpoche.

Although the story of my taking Refuge into the Buddhist tradition with Kalu Rinpoche at this time has its own flavor of magic, I focus here on my interactions with the wild Dane, Ole, and his band of traveling Dharma warriors.

My first direct encounter with Ole was in the Samye Ling dining room. Dharma centers can be quite serious and sometimes even sanctimonious. And meal times at Samye Ling were no exception. People sat at benches eating in reflective states of mind - except for all of these Danes and Germans who beamed health and joy as they joked with each other.

I have learned over the years that such a joyous demeanor is one of the fruits of meditation practice. And much of this natural expression of joy is encouraged by Ole, who, as it happened, passed directly behind me as I sat appreciating my brown rice and vegetables. He stopped, placed both his hands on my shoulders and pressed his thumbs deep into my trapezius muscles with a fair amount of force. For whatever reason, I made no remark, nor did I flinch, even though I did feel a fair amount of pain as he kept his thumbs pressed in. When that magical, eternal moment had passed and he released the pressure, his only comment was, "Hmm. Not bad." No more was said and aside from a class where he gave the visualization on the Bodhisattva of Compassion, Chenrezig, I had no further interaction with Ole while at Samye Ling.

Four weeks later, Kalu Rinpoche was giving a Chenrezig empowerment at the Quaker Meeting House in central London. There were, I would say, 300 people present. Being in the presence of such a master who was also my refuge lama was wonderful. With good feelings and after a meaningful empowerment, I decided to leave the hall as people milled around and purchased malas and incense from the vendors who are always at such events.

The hallways of the Quaker Meeting House are quite long and when you walk along them alone, the echo of your footsteps resounds. It was perhaps three-quarters down the hall that I began to hear the sound of running coming from behind. Not thinking that it had anything to do with me, I continued towards the door when, suddenly, a familiar hand was on my shoulder turning me around. I came face to face with Ole, who was already in the process of tying a red plastic protection cord around my neck. Looking into my eyes, he only said, "We'll meet again in the future." Somewhat dazed and obviously more confused than he, all I could say was, "If you say so."

Five years later in Woodstock, New York when His Holiness Karmapa was visiting, we had our reunion. We were like friends or brothers who had not seen each other for years. There was an immediate recognition and sense of celebration between us. And that is how it has been since 1980. Wherever Melanie and I have lived, once and sometimes twice a year Ole has traveled there, bringing an ever increasing entourage of Dharma students from Europe, teaching, conferring blessings and then moving off again in the middle of the night to continue his ritual journeying across America to do what he is best at doing - inspiring friends and strangers alike to practice Dharma.

Over the years and because of our connection through His Holiness, I had grown more and more perceptive as to when Ole was nearing where we lived. This certainly didn't have to do with agreed upon or approximate times of arrival. Ole travels in the fast lane. Sometimes he will leave one place at 1 a.m. after a teaching; sometimes the next day, after he and his friends have perused all the available thrift and army-navy stores in a region. Regardless, even if he arrives breathless, he has never been late for a teaching engagement. His arrival on January 16th was no different.

As had become my custom since Shamara's birth, I awoke early and took her upstairs with me to do my practice. Midway through our time in the shrine room, I felt a familiar feeling; the feeling that let me know that Ole was in the vicinity of Lexington. And, as usual, it was within moments of completing my practice that the phone rang. It was Ole, letting me know that he had stopped on the outskirts of Lexington with his friends to get some breakfast after an all-night drive from New York.

While it was still early morning hours, Melanie was soon up, as were Kai and Tina. And by about 6:30 a.m. Ole had arrived with his band of Danes and Germans. What Melanie and I noticed most about this particular group was that - as they came one at a time through our front door - each traveler was taller than the preceding one. Even Ole's travel companion, Edita, seemed like a giant. And the largest was Burkhardt - indeed a gentle giant to whom our daughter Tina was immediately drawn. All of the travelers needed to rest. Some were to stay with us while others would stay with friends.

Besides all the comings and goings of people wanting to see Ole, a friend and psychic, John Kane, had arranged for Ole to be his guest on a local talk radio program in nearby

Nicholasville, Kentucky. John was usually unaccompanied as he provided his psychic services to callers. He now had the added energy of Ole being broadcast into the Kentucky hills. Ole performed divinations for callers and answered their questions with a candor and directness that - without a doubt - shocked some of John's listening audience. I remember one caller who asked about an illness she was having and Ole suggested she visualize a blue Buddha in front of her - the Medicine Buddha. I will never forget how - in her thick Kentuckiana accent - she repeated, "Right, I visualize a blue Buddha."

Evening came around quickly. Our friends Ann Frye and Dick Levine had arranged for Ole to speak at the university. While I prepared sound equipment, cushions and the various bits and pieces needed for the evening, Melanie bathed Shamara with the help of Edita. Edita had grown particularly close to Shamara throughout the day and looked softened by having the opportunity to help one so young. Kai and Tina were to stay with friends while the rest of us went off to the talk.

The topic was the Four Noble Truths as taught by the Buddha. And one of Ole's greatest gifts is to be able to articulate such profound teachings in a way that touches people in their everyday experience of life. This is precisely what he did that evening with clarity, gentleness and humor.

It is one of those rare circumstances when both parents of an infant can sit together in a public event with the infant present and not find at least one of them tending to whatever needs arise. Shamara sat quietly for almost all of Ole's presentation. It was only towards the end, when he had opened up the talk to questions from the audience that Shamara became noticeably agitated and began to cry.

As she had not been nursed in a while, Melanie decided to leave the room and see if she could settle her. But Shamara persisted in crying and seemed inconsolable. More than half an hour went by and her crying remained unchanged. After Ole finished his presentation and we were closing up the room, we came out into the hallway to find Melanie still wearily pacing back and forth with Shamara.

Down in the parking lot, in the car, all the way home, Shamara's tears continued relentlessly and Melanie's anxiety and tension heightened. By the time we arrived home, Melanie was nearly beside herself. In such times - although they had never been so extreme - we would gently bundle Shamara up, lay her in her carry cot and place her in our shrine room. This always quieted her down faster than anything else and if she awakened, we could easily hear her from our bedroom. Tonight was no exception as once Melanie set Shamara in the shrine room, her tears subsided. Soon she was quiet. And for the first time in nearly 90 minutes, Melanie and I could sit down and spend time with Ole and our friends.

By 1:30 in the morning all of us had become sufficiently tired to get to sleep. There had not been a sound from upstairs and rather than tempt fate, Melanie just listened from the doorway instead of going up the stairs to check on

Shamara. As any parent of a newborn baby knows, that first full night of sleep after the baby is born is an eagerly awaited pleasure. It seemed that tonight might be the night. Heavy with tiredness and having no thought that anything untoward was taking place, we went to bed. And the night became still.

CHAPTER SEVEN

DEATH AND REBIRTH

lthough I had gotten to bed later than usual, I still found myself awake at my regular hour.

Though I had slept deeply, just before rising I had a dream that so disturbed me that I felt as if all of the hairs on my body had been standing on end during the dream.

In the dream I was lying on my back in bed. Toward me, from the side door of the bedroom, walked a toothless, middle-aged hag with long black hair. Her mouth was twisted open to one side and she was dressed in a red T-shirt with Tibetan calligraphy on the front. She swayed as she walked and her cackle was blood curdling. The air around her was deathly cold. She came closer and closer until, finally, she was leaning over me, still cackling. And it was while looking up at her that I literally shook myself from sleep.

At that moment I made no real effort to determine the significance of the dream. It was morning and what seemed most significant was that Melanie and I had had our first full - albeit short - night's rest since Shamara's birth. After washing, I made my way up to the shrine room where Shamara's cot was. She was lying very still, face down in her cot. Even though she often slept like this, I found myself experiencing a pang of apprehension. I felt the back of her neck with the back of my hand. It was warm to my touch. And, oddly enough, I was surprised. I dismissed my feeling of apprehension. After all, had not both Melanie and I been dealing with such feelings almost every day of Shamara's life?

Thinking that I mustn't wake her too soon (lest I catch the wrath of a peacefully sleeping mother), I picked up Shamara's cot and moved it downstairs to the kitchen, where I assumed that once she stirred, Melanie would hear her and come to tend to her needs.

I began my morning meditation practice as usual, yet, at the same time, remained hyper-attentive as I waited for the sounds of Melanie rousing and coming to Shamara. I noted within myself how each moment was vivid and full - the way I usually get when something powerful is about to happen in my life.

Meanwhile, with the initial sounds of my meditation bells, Melanie awakened. As she lay there in bed, rather than savoring the feeling of being well-rested, her mind immediately went to thoughts of whether or not Shamara was alive. Both of us had dealt with these thoughts again and again; had put them out of our minds again and again. This time, however, Melanie allowed herself to dwell on them - to take them even further. What would she do if she found Shamara dead? First off, she thought, she would call our friend Gary Heinz, who was a carpenter. She would ask Gary to make a small pine coffin for Shamara. Who else would need to be contacted?

In order to shake herself free from these morbid thoughts, Melanie decided to get up and come to the shrine room to get Shamara. As she walked to the kitchen to open the door to the shrine room, she caught sight of Shamara's carry cot near the washing machine. Melanie was relieved with the thought that I had obviously checked Shamara to see that she was alright. Why else would I have brought her cot down to the kitchen?

I heard Melanie moving about downstairs and I was relieved, knowing that she was now with Shamara. And as quickly as that relief arose it was shattered with the sounds of Melanie's screams - screams which in an instant made me totally aware of what had happened.

I leaped down the stairs to find Melanie, half crouching, stiff, holding Shamara in her arms and screaming "Something is wrong!" I grabbed Shamara. She was stiff and cold and as I turned her over I saw that the whole left side of her face was blue and compressed. Mucous had hardened below her nose and on her upper lip and her mouth was twisted open - just like the hag in my dream.

It was obvious that she was dead. Yet somehow, Melanie and I wanted to deny the truth of what we were seeing. There was a feeling of total impotence. And, it was in that state of mental anguish and confusion that I ran with Shamara in my arms to Ole's room and burst in the door.

Ole met me right at the door. He had gotten up and was coming to us after hearing Melanie's screams. Holding Shamara's stiff body out to him, shaking, I shouted, "Do something!" Without a moment's hesitation and with a commanding directness he looked at me, took Shamara and said, "All right." He then went upstairs to the shrine room, sat down in front of the altar, placed Shamara upright on his lap and began the prayers for Phowa.

In the Tibetan Buddhist tradition, it is important to do spiritual practice during one's life for several reasons. First and foremost, by creating positive impressions in our minds through prayer and meditation focused with altruistic intentions, we become more open, dynamic and creative. Compassion toward others naturally arises. The second reason practice is so important is that it creates the seeds for a more positive rebirth by helping us to die more consciously. Phowa is a traditional practice that is particularly useful at the time of dying.

In Phowa, the meditator visualizes his or her body in a certain way and focuses attention on energies moving in the body. Through concentration, visualization and primordial sounds, this energy is gathered, concentrated, focused, aimed and shot out of the body through the psychic aperture in the crown of the head. (This is the area called the "soft spot" on a young child or the crown chakra in Eastern spiritual traditions.)

This is important because the crown chakra is the doorway or conduit through which spiritual energy enters and leaves one's being. It is from here that the energy can most efficiently leave in order to move towards a better incarnation or rebirth. If the energy were to move out of one of the other chakras or if it were to exit the body elsewhere due to shock, trauma or accident, then the next incarnation, though it might be in keeping with some of the individual's karmic tendencies, would in no way provide that individual with the opportunity for the most beneficial rebirth possible.

Rather than being reborn into circumstances and opportunities which would foster increased spiritual development, the individual would be caught up in more gross, mundane expressions of resolved or unresolved feelings and hopes, dreams and desires, perhaps even being reborn in a less fortunate realm than that of humans, such as that of animals or ghosts. Buddhism teaches that while we do possess Buddha nature, unfoldment into that nature does not necessarily follow a linear path. The manner in which we use our potential in any given life determines what subsequent lives will have in store for us.

In Phowa, the focus and aim of the practice is for us to propel ourselves into the heart of the Amitabha Buddha and thus be born into Dewachen, the Western Pure Land of Amitabha. In this Pure Land, one has the opportunity to develop spiritually without hindrance. And once realization or enlightenment is firmly established, one can then consciously manifest in whatever realm seems most beneficial to help others still caught in suffering.

Although I describe these ideas and the goal here in Buddhist terms, understanding how to focus one's psychic energy in the way it is taught in Phowa is also effective for anyone who can focus and aim his or her psychic force towards a deity or being in whom confidence is felt, such as God, Jesus or Mohammed.

Traditionally, Phowa is practiced in retreat with other yogic energy practices. However, it is also taught to lay persons over the course of their lives so that at the time of dying, as the positive habit of focusing, aiming and moving the energy through the body has been established, it will naturally and spontaneously occur.

When someone who has never learned the Phowa practice is dying or has just died, a lama is asked to perform the practice. The reason this is possible is that the psychic energy in the body does not leave immediately. Initially what happens is that, as the elements of the body dissolve, the psychic energy moves towards the heart. As long as there is heat around the heart of the deceased, the psychic force is still present.

The length of time this heat remains depends upon the individual's spiritual development. If there is little development, the heat may leave within a few hours. For the average person it takes about three days, which is probably why so many indigenous cultures have customarily left the body alone for that length of time. This is also why autopsies and emergency procedures which alter the body's natural release of energy are discouraged. (However, many teachers believe that the act of donating one's vital organs so that another person can live has a very positive effect on future rebirths.)

With great masters, the psychic energy can remain in the body for as long as 49 days. This was indeed the case with His Holiness, the 16th Karmapa, who was able to propel his heart out of his cremation fire after 49 days - a sign to all of his mastery and enlightenment. A Phowa master working with someone who does not have such ability or practice experience can, through touch and sound vibration, literally shoot the psychic force out of the body and into the heart of Amitabha.

A true Phowa adept can do this even for someone whose psychic force has left the body in a less than beneficial manner by visualizing the individual and making certain prayers to bring the soul back in, so to speak, and then re-releasing that individual to the Pure Land. This particular accomplishment demands a very high level of skill and power from the Phowa master.

There are physical signs that appear on the body when the transference of consciousness has taken place. In retreat or when practicing Phowa, the adept will develop a spot of blood or red, sore spot on the crown of the head, or will have a spontaneous stream of pure fluid pour from the nostrils. This is the outer sign that the energy has been moved properly.

So here we were, with a lama and Phowa master actually in our house as our daughter died. And the heat that I had felt at the back of her neck was a sign that her psychic energy was still in her body.

Ole remained upstairs with Shamara. Edita and another German friend, Wolfgang, went up to be with Ole and to practice. Meanwhile, I needed to be downstairs. Kai and Tina had been awakened by Melanie's screams. They found their mother trembling from the shock of what she had just experienced. Burkhardt, who had also stayed overnight, helped Melanie, and I consoled the children, all the while trying to gain some clarity within myself as to what to say and do next.

The girls heard the chanting upstairs and knowing that it had something to do with their little sister, wanted to go up and see her. How does one explain to a three year old child and a five year old child that their little sister is dead? Holding them close to us, Melanie and I could only say to them that Shamara had left us. We told them that Ole was helping her and that they could see her in a little while. This is the best we could do.

Here, Burkhardt showed the depth of his compassion. This giant of a man, was especially able to calm and ease the mind of little three year old Tina.

Meanwhile, I felt the need to call Walt Stoll. I could hear him begin to cry over the phone as I gave him the news. For him, Shamara's birth had been the most beautiful and powerful birthing he had ever been a part of. And now this. He mustered enough composure to give us professional advice as to what steps we would need to take. The first thing I needed to do was to get in touch with the coroner's office.

Within a half-hour of calling, the deputy coroner arrived. He was a young, graceful man with a moustache. He was well-trained at being the bearer of bad tidings. He demonstrated a natural, gentle quality of empathy as he entered the house. Of course, he wanted to see Shamara and I had to explain to him in some way what basically was going on upstairs. I led him upstairs and he remained for a few minutes while Ole continued the Phowa. He then came downstairs and sat, saying that he would wait for the ceremony to end. In the meantime, he called the police photographer who arrived shortly thereafter.

In this time, I also made a call to Karma Triyana Dharmachakra, where I presumed my teacher, Khenpo Karthar Rinpoche was. The secretary told me that Khenpo Rinpoche was in New York City and that I would have to call him at the meditation center there. When I made that call I learned that, in fact, Rinpoche was not at the center but somewhere in the city, so I would have to call at a later time. I left a message of what had happened.

From the time Ole began Phowa and I started through the ordeal of telling our daughters, Walt, the deputy coroner and the police photographer and trying to contact Khenpo Rinpoche, a little over an hour passed. There was a feeling of chaotic heaviness that made each moment seem eternal. This atmosphere was broken as Ole called Melanie and me upstairs in what sounded like a completely joyful tone of voice.

He had placed Shamara on her back in her little carry-cot and both Melanie and I looked at her in amazement. The blueness had left her face, her mouth was normal and her appearance peaceful, almost radiant. And, from her nose there was streaming a clear fluid. This fluid had been preceded by a long strand of white foam which Ole and Edita watched being literally propelled out of her nose at the moment when Ole had felt the transference of Shamara's consciousness taking place. Although Melanie and I did not witness this, just knowing how Shamara had looked when we found her and seeing her now after Phowa was convincing enough. Our daughter had, indeed, been reborn into Amitabha's Pure Land!

Theoretically, we understood what had happened, but the reality of it was hard to grasp in the moment. It would have been easy to remain transfixed by the miracle. However, we were compelled to deal with other mundane but necessary issues.

We called the deputy coroner who was completely astounded since, just half an hour before, he had seen Shamara's cold, blue, distorted appearance. The photographer also came upstairs, but, since he did not realize what had happened, he simply took her photos and departed.

When the coroner and photographer were finished, we called Tina and Kai. With tears in their eyes and acting very bravely, they came upstairs to say good-bye to Shamara. Ever so delicately, they kissed her cheek and were then led downstairs by Edita and Burkhardt. Ole produced a relic from the Kumboom stupa and placed it in the bonnet that she still wore. I went downstairs to get the red T-shirt with Tibetan calligraphy that I had gotten the last time I was in New York. It was the same one that the hag had worn in my dream. It was Shamara's and I wanted her to be cremated with it.

Ole told me that the deputy coroner could take Shamara's body - that it was now an empty vessel. I was still in disbelief of what had happened and admittedly was not as certain of Ole's ability in Phowa as I now am. I wanted Khenpo Rinpoche to say that it was all right to let her go.

This time when I called, Tenzin Chonyi, President of KTD and then one of the translators for Khenpo Rinpoche answered the phone. He said that Rinpoche had confirmed that the transference had occurred. Rinpoche and Ole then talked for a few minutes about what had happened. Melanie then got on the phone with Tenzin who began speaking in a most understanding way. He told Melanie that normally he does not remember dreams but, that night, the night Shamara had passed, he had a dream that a small child was reborn into Dewachen.

With Tenzin and Rinpoche's words I now felt prepared to let the deputy coroner take Shamara. Still wrapped in her night clothes and bonnet, with a piece of a stupa at her crown and a red T-shirt with the Tibetan symbol for Kalachakra, he carried her cot to the car and drove off. We waved good-bye from the porch. Later on we heard from the deputy coroner. The coroner's report was that the autopsy revealed that Shamara had been in excellent health. It was also evident that she had been well cared for. His diagnosis was that she had died of SIDS.

Birth and - we now learned - death are primordial events. They occur all the time, yet they are extraordinary in how they make it effortless to drop what is superfluous from one's life and make one focus in the here and now of what truly needs to be done. No doubt such attention and action is facilitated by the blanket of shock that one is physically and psychically experiencing at such times.

Kai and Tina needed baths. Edita and Burkhardt tended to them. Melanie and I called our respective parents. Melanie's parents, being in Britain, could only grieve with us from a distance. My parents, from whom I had been estranged for some time, responded immediately by saying that they were on their way from Florida to be with us. The house needed to be cleaned. We were still in the middle of Ole's visit. People would be calling for appointments. Then there was the fact that we had made a public announcement about a talk by Ole at our house that night. Not knowing who would come, we decided to let it all happen. And, we were hungry.

I had been told by others that death can make one hungry. And no doubt for all of us, that was true as we seemed to eat an enormous volume of food at a hotel-all-you-can-eat salad bar. It did not feel like we were eating to hold down feelings. In fact, life felt so vivid, so clear. There was a tremendous sense of caring among all of us there; Ole, Edita, Burkhardt, other German friends, Melanie, myself, Kai and Tina. And it was in this state of mind that Ole told us a story about another little girl that he knew.

An American couple had given birth to a little girl a few years before. When she turned two years of age, her parents decided that they wanted to take her with them on a trip to Thailand to see Southeast Asia, especially the great Thai Buddhist temples.

Once they had toured Thailand and other parts of Southeast Asia, they decided to go to Sikkim to see their teacher, the Karmapa. They had been at Rumtek, the monastery of the Karmapa, just one night when, during the night, their daughter died.

This was clearly not a case of SIDS as SIDS is medically considered to occur only to children less than one year of age. Totally beside themselves with grief they went to the Karmapa to ask him what had gone wrong.

The Karmapa looked at them and smiled. He told them that nothing had gone wrong. Still they wanted a reason. And so he gave them one. His Holiness had known their daughter in her previous life. She had been a very famous religious adept, a yogini. When she was dying, she apparently told His Holiness that in her next life all she wanted to do was see a few of the great temples of Thailand and that would be enough. In this lifetime, her parents fulfilled her request. And she could then leave.

Our own daughter was born into an atmosphere still charged with the blessing of our teacher, Khenpo Karthar Rinpoche. She heard mantras at birth and heard prayers daily. Her last night alive was at a Dharma talk. And, she died in the presence of a lama and Phowa Master.

Years later I learned the significance of my dream of the hag. A Tibetan doctor and monk explained that a hag in a dream signifies that life is being taken away to another place - a reminder that life goes on and that death is the shroud it must don in order to move from one place to the next. In Shamara's case, a Pure Land.

CHAPTER EIGHT

TEN DAYS OF MIRACLES

I have learned over the years from my conversation with others who have been in the presence of death, that they witnessed omens and signs before and after the time of dying. For these people such occurrences were miraculous and transformative. In actual fact, I believe such occurrences are normal; they happen all the time. It is just a matter of how awake one is at the time they take place. It seems that life is constantly giving us opportunities to wake up, become conscious - to see clearly what is and is not important in the course of our lives.

Having said that, let me also say that I do not consider myself to be very awake at all. However, the events that took place over the next 10 days after Shamara's passing were so blatant that Melanie and I would have to have been comatose not to see them as miracles and opportunities to awaken to a deeper level of spiritual reality.

After returning home from lunch at the hotel, there were more mundane affairs to be tended to. There was still going to be a talk by Ole at our home that evening. We had to clean and prepare for whomever would appear at our door. By this time, the morning's occurrences had been passed on via the community grapevine. We knew that some of our friends would be coming, almost as if to a funeral service. There would also be others who were not aware of what had happened and were simply expecting to come to a special Dharma talk. And there were Melanie, the children and myself; tired, in shock, in pain and strangely filled with joy at knowing what had taken place for Shamara.

The talk was at 7:30 and people began to arrive at 7:00. It was obvious from facial expressions who knew and who didn't. Death is not a word that we like to use in social settings. So to those who were not aware of what had happened, it must have seemed bizarre to see others come in tearful, sad, wanting to give hugs and be close.

It was actually rather strange. Both Melanie and I felt that much of what we needed to do was to comfort these people. They were seemingly here for us, but on a deeper level, Shamara's passing had evoked deep feelings and questions in all of them.

When 7:30 came around and everyone was gathered upstairs in the shrine room, Ole, Melanie and I went up and sat in front of what must have been 50 people.

I had told people that the talk for the evening was going to be different than what we had advertised. It was going to be about death, impermanence and the importance of Dharma practice in our lives. And I told them why we had changed the program.

A visible shudder went through the room as my words telling them about Shamara's passing sank in. Everyone's breathing became deeper. And while some eyes filled with tears, others simply stared forward in discomfort - as if something were being evoked for which they were not prepared. In the presence of the energy of Phowa, so much love was present that it seemed as if each friend were being honored by whatever he or she was experiencing in those moments. And in that atmosphere, Ole began his talk which was both moving and direct in its message. We all became engulfed in the sacredness of the moment.

Ole always does a meditation at the end of his talks and on this evening, he gave the visualization on Mikyo Dorje, the 8th Karmapa. Ole has mastered the timing and presentation of guided meditations and his voice seemed to create an atmosphere of blessing energy flowing down from the Karmapa. In fact, his image was that of snow-flakes descending around us and filling our entire bodies.

The warmth and caring we all felt in that room made it seem as if we could remain there forever. Any thought of parting for the evening seemed unreal. As people came down from the shrine room, many came to Melanie and me. So many of them had been deeply touched by the evening, so much so that one friend, who had recently had an abortion, told us that if she ever got pregnant again, knowing how uncertain the course of life is, that she would definitely keep the child and do her best to bring it into the world. Another group of friends had gotten together to give us some money so that Melanie and I could take some time off work. Our friend and midwife, Noni, returned our check for her services as midwife in Shamara's birth. Though Melanie protested, Noni was so earnestly insistent that we accepted. Ironically the amount Noni returned to us was exactly the cost for Shamara's cremation. Another friend had the unusual request of wanting Melanie to express breast milk for a niece of hers who was dying of leukemia. Melanie obliged.

Many other friends told us that they would be in touch with us to help out in any way that they could. So many friends we had made in Lexington. And in true friendship, it seemed, they were opening their hearts to us. Evenings with Ole always run late and, finally, everyone was gone and the house was quiet. The night was clear and mild.

Morning came around silently - a new experience as both Melanie and I had gotten used to Shamara's stirrings. It was a reminder to us that the passing had not been a dream.

The light of dawn was just appearing. As I passed the dining room windows, I looked out to find the entire neighborhood covered in a velvet blanket of pure white snow. This was such a contrast to what the weather of the previous days and even the night before had been. And, in an instant, I recalled Ole's meditation on the blessing of Mikyo Dorje descending upon us like flakes of snow. My heart was comforted by seeing nature in synchronicity with sacred vision and our aspirations. In such a state of mind I went up to the shrine room.

Normally I would have emptied the bowls of the shrine

before going to sleep. I had been just too tired to be bothered with it so late the night before. Thus I was aware that I needed to empty the bowls and prepare them anew before beginning my practice for the day. I was not prepared for what I saw.

Many of the bowls of water were almost empty, still upright. Food offerings that had been on the shrine were not there or just a small amount was remaining. Being the last one in the shrine room for the night, I was totally certain that no one visiting from the night before had gone and helped themselves to these offerings. We had no mice that I was aware of and it wasn't hot enough for such an amount of water to have evaporated. Therefore, my mind came around to what seemed a possible but somewhat miraculous conclusion: that dakinis and other deity beings to whom we make such offerings had actually come and accepted our offering to them!

Being in an atmosphere that was evidently saturated with blessing and in a state where solid reality was quite obviously being transformed in our minds, I was at once joyful and amazed, yet at the same time, quite calm and accepting of such manifestations. Ole, Melanie, Edita and others had similar reactions.

It was soon after practice that friends began to call. Some had talked the night before about wanting to learn more about Phowa. Others were calling now for the same reason. I spoke with Ole and he agreed to get together with all those interested to teach the visualization for Phowa. And at 11 a.m. the morning of January 18th, Ole taught the visualization for Phowa for the first time in the United States. This was to be the first of many gatherings where Ole has fulfilled the wishes of his teacher, the Venerable Tenga Rinpoche, to teach Phowa in the West.

Melanie and I were almost in a state of suspended animation for the next few days. And Ole, Edita and Burkhardt stayed with us as friends and guides. They were joined by Geoff and Diana who had grown keenly aware of what Khenpo Rinpoche had requested of them only eight weeks ago. It was they, in fact, who kept our daily lives together, helping us with meals, sorting out mail and doing whatever was needed to keep ordinary life moving forward. Kai and Tina went back to school, but we allowed them to come home any time if they felt shaky or just wanted to stay close to us.

It was on January 20th in the morning that Ole departed with Edita, Burkhardt and a few of the others in the entourage who had stayed on in Lexington for those few days. We had grown close to each one of them and over the years our reunions with them have been filled with a special warmth and appreciation. As for Ole, our love and appreciation for his commitment to His Holiness and the Dharma and what he had done for Shamara made our connection to him diamond-like - indestructible.

Since these times much has transpired in transmitting Dharma to the West and some have come to question Ole and his methods of teaching Dharma. From his own perspective of nearly 25 years of studying and living with Tibetans, Ole is strongly committed to ensuring that the

Dharma - and especially Vajrayana Buddhism as preserved by the Tibetan people - does not become sullied by Communist Chinese aggression and interference in Tibet's culture or politics. Knowing him as we do and having the special connection that has obviously traversed the boundaries of time, we remain steadfast as friends, students and fellow travelers along the path of Dharma.

After Ole left, my parents arrived from Florida. It is not unusual for death to bring a family closer together. Issues of attitude and lifestyle which might have generated heated discussion at other times seem petty in the face of death. Thus it was that the healing process between us began.

What seemed to bring this about was my mother's and father's observation of how Melanie and I were handling ourselves and Kai and Tina. Because we had received so many concerned calls and visits from friends, I decided to make a tape recording of the events that took place and how Melanie and I viewed them so that we would not have to repeat ourselves constantly. Months later my mother was to comment that letting them listen to that tape helped them a great deal in understanding us as well as the practice of Buddhism.

My mother helped watch Kai and Tina and my father, in his characteristic way, remained a silent, powerful support. It was he who drove us to the coroner's office to pick up Shamara's ashes. It felt eerie to be holding a plastic container with the cremated remains of the tiny baby we had held in our arms only days before.

We had already decided to mail the ashes to Shamar Rinpoche in India. Ole had said that it was traditional for lamas to be given the ashes of the deceased. They would dispose of or use them in ceremonial ways and this seemed the most fitting use for Shamara's ashes. The trip to the post office, mailing the package, driving home - all were done in a dream-like state. My father's love and care in those hours held a warmth that nurtured both Melanie and me.

I had not yet returned to work. And the calls kept coming in as did flowers, cards, food and whatever forms of care and support friends could offer. But what was also apparent to us was how much pain everyone around us was in. After talking with my parents and Geoff and Diana, it seemed that the best thing for us would be to go away for a while. Thus it was that Melanie and I decided to go to visit Khenpo Rinpoche in Woodstock, New York.

The day Melanie, Kai, Tina and I left Lexington was overcast and cold. The energy and blessing of the time around Shamara's transference seemed to fade into the darkness of our sense of loss. The weather accurately reflected our mood. Fifteen miles north of Lexington I was stopped for speeding. Normally I would have chatted with the officer in the hopes that my friendliness would let us get off with a warning. But I couldn't be bothered. As if the ticket were just part of what the darkness was offering, I accepted it and drove off.

We had decided that Kai and Tina would be better served by staying with our dear friends, Charles and Deborah Dawes and their three children, Daniel, Jonathan and Rosemary. We had been friends in the Columbus, Ohio

Buddhist community and our children were of similar ages. Kai and Tina liked the idea as did the Dawes family. We only spent a short time getting the children settled in before Melanie and I were on our way to Woodstock.

This was an unusual situation for Melanie and me - for there to be just the two of us, alone and on the road. It was a relief not to have to relate to anyone else. We did not speak very much. Occasionally we just held hands. Silence and touch were all that was needed.

By our calculations, it would be midnight by the time we got to the monastery. Rinpoche was happy we were coming and Ngodrup Burkhar had let Tenzin Chonyi know that as he, Marianne and their daughter, Kalsang, were out of town that Melanie and I could use their cabin for the duration of our stay. It was a short distance from the monastery's main building. The privacy would be most welcome.

As we traveled along Interstate 80 at dusk, it became more and more obvious with each mile that we were driving into a winter storm front. Small flakes of snow hitting the windshield became larger and more constant. Drifts swirled toward the car as the wind speed increased. I had been raised in Cleveland, so driving in such conditions was not unfamiliar. We pressed on.

By 11:30 p.m., with more and more ice on the road and travel speed greatly reduced, we knew that we would be much longer than anticipated. Both of us felt alert. There seemed to be no point in stopping; just go with things as they were. We were now traveling about 35 miles per hour along the freeway. Visibility was down to less than 10 feet. It was hard to know where the lanes were, since we could only use our low beam lights as the brights only intensified the glare off the snow.

Both Melanie and I were silent and focusing on the road. It was in that frame of mind that the silence was shattered by a large truck passing us on the right side, going at least double our speed. The size and speed of this truck blinded us with more snow and the tail wind made the car begin to swerve. And no sooner had this happened than on the left, another truck passed, going even faster.

The combined force of the tail winds and snow thrown by both trucks reduced our visibility to zero and made steering impossible. We were fish-tailing wildly down the road with each yard feeling like it would lead us into a total spin. Trying to brake and adjust my steering was not even a consideration. In that moment - where there seemed no choice - I let go of the wheel completely. Melanie and I braced ourselves for what seemed to be a fatal situation.

In the space of those moments sliding down the freeway out of control, a force like a large hand coming out of the sky seemed to grab the car. No sooner had Melanie and I felt this presence, than, for no apparent reason, the car began moving in a straight line down the road again. The steering wheel had stopped spinning. I was once again able to place my hands on it. And it was as if nothing unusual had happened.

We drove on for a few minutes until we saw arrows pointing to a roadside rest area. I pulled into a parking space and turned off the engine. And we just sat looking at each other. "What happened?" Melanie asked sheepishly. I certainly had no answer; at least no answer that would make sense in three-dimensional, linear, rational reality. Somehow, we both knew that a presence beyond our normal senses had just prevented us from dying in the middle of the night on the Pennsylvania thruway.

Later on, as we talked about what had happened in those few seconds, it seemed that we had both faced them in a similar mind state. It was as if a gap had appeared for us. We were totally open and in that open space, we had both silently chanted the mantra, "Karmapa Cheno." And since we had both silently and spontaneously chanted the mantra of Karmapa, we felt that it was his blessing that had made this miracle arise.

In that moment we took only a short time to reflect on our blessing. Even though the road was getting worse, even though we had just had a brush with death, the power of this event gave us the resolve to keep going - to get to our spiritual home and be with our spiritual father.

Darkness gave way to light as we drove on through the stormy night. Passing through the town of Woodstock in the early morning, we were virtually the only car on the road. Here, too, it was bleak, gray and stormy with roads covered in slush and ice. We decided to use the less steep, back road up to the monastery as we were concerned that the front road would be impassable.

As we wearily drove those last few miles up that road, we became enveloped in the same cloud cover which shrouded the mountain on whose crest the monastery is situated. It seemed that all of the gray and the darkness of the preceding night was culminating on these slopes. Then, as if in a dream, as we approached the summit where Karma Triyana sits, the entire sky opened up before us. The clouds melted away, the sky was a deep blue and the monastery and snow covered land around it were vivid in the dazzling light. It was a glorious sight. Our 21 hour journey had come to an end. I parked the car and, with a sigh, we got out.

Morning meditation on the Protectress Green Tara was just finishing as Melanie and I sat, drinking a cup of tea in the monastery dining room. It wasn't but a few minutes till Khenpo Rinpoche walked in. Never straying from total awareness, he came in silently, seeming to not even disturb the particles of dust in the air. His gaze was one of pain and benevolence as he came toward us and embraced us one at a time. In his arms, Melanie was able to weep openly for the first time since Shamara's passing. Rinpoche indicated that we could get together with him in the afternoon. For now, we were to eat, settle in and rest.

The morning passed while Melanie and I rested. It felt as though we had not slept in weeks.

In the afternoon of that first day we met with Rinpoche and Tenzin. We talked with Rinpoche about the Phowa and expressed our interest in pursuing its study and practice. There were preliminary practices he wanted us to do to ensure that we would see the benefits of doing Phowa. He also gave us some protective visualizations to use in the practice, for if done improperly, one's life force can be dissipated rapidly while practicing Phowa.

He also told us in a tone that I have come to never question that what had happened to us with Shamara would not happen again were we to have another child. Here he was not addressing the miracle that had taken place, but the ordinary Melanie and me who felt the pain and loss.

Rinpoche's prayers are powerful and we felt a new strength enter us as he spoke and prayed over us. He then presented us with one of his personal shrine statues. It was of Green Tara, the protectress who was formed from the tear of the great Bodhisattva, Chenrezig. To this day, she sits prominently on our altar. We make prayers to her.

In the warmth of the love Khenpo Rinpoche had shown us, the days that followed were uneventful, save that they were quite nurturing; sleeping without interruption, preparing simple meals in Ngodrup and Marianne's kitchen, meditating, taking walks to the Magic Meadow, visiting friends and helping with monastery chores as needed.

The weather had grown colder and more snow covered the mountain. Periodically we ventured into town; but by the 5th day, unless one had a truck or a four-wheel drive, leaving the monastery was neither practical nor safe. Looking back on this time, it has become apparent to both Melanie and me that invisible forces were once again at work. The cold and snow slowed us down, encouraged us to take time, to allow ourselves to be nurtured and to prepare for what was to come next. It was now 10 days since Shamara's passing.

On that 10th day, Melanie and I had reluctantly driven down to Woodstock for some items we needed. There had been a plan for us to have dinner with some friends in town, but they were cancelled at the last moment and it was actually a relief to be heading back to the quiet safety of the little cabin we had been living in. The snow was becoming heavier and we were happy to park the car for the day. As we left the car, we observed several friends coming in and out of the lama's house in a somewhat frantic state.

We were told by one friend, Flo, that Saima, another of the monastery residents, was about ready to give birth. She asked if I would be prepared to drive her to the hospital. Melanie and I did not know Saima, but doing that for her was no problem. Still, we wanted to meet Saima, to see how she was doing.

We entered into Saima's room in the basement of the lama's house. In her early 40s, she was a vibrant woman of Finnish extraction, very steely, yet soft and radiant at the same time. And she was very definitely in the latter stages of labor.

A call had been put through to her doctor. Saima wanted him to come to the monastery to birth the baby there, but he was insistent that she meet him at the hospital. Saima's labor had gone fast up to this point and she was not convinced that she would make it to the hospital on time with weather conditions as they were.

Her fear was compounded by the fact that her own mother had hemorrhaged and died when Saima was being delivered. The thought of being without medical support terrified her. She hoped that if she just held out, the doctor would see that there was no choice but to come. The problem was that with every passing minute, the roads leading to town became more and more treacherous. Melanie and I talked it over and it was decided that she would stay with Saima to help with the labor. Hopefully, one more call to the doctor would convince him to come to the monastery. In case it became clear that this wasn't going to happen and birth was imminent, Melanie would call me at Ngodrup's house to come get Saima in the car and take her to the hospital.

I decided to make myself useful by preparing the evening meal for Melanie and me. However, it wasn't even 20 minutes until I got the call. In that short time Melanie could see that Saima was going through transition. If she was going to be transported at all, it had to happen now. As a precaution, Flo had called the paramedic unit to come up to the monastery if we couldn't get out.

I dropped the back seat on our Pinto wagon, put a mattress inside to make Saima less uncomfortable and pulled around to the lama's house. Walking into the room where Saima was, however, made me change my mind about transporting her. I had been through three home births with Melanie and was very familiar with what a woman looks like when the baby is about to come.

In a moment of calm in the storm of contractions, I asked Saima if she would mind me checking her vaginally to see where the baby's head was. (In such times, modesty is not a primary consideration.) She consented and reaching in I found - not to my surprise - that the baby's head was crowning. "Saima," I said, "you're not going anywhere. We're going to do this right here and now."

While Melanie helped Saima relax her breathing, I massaged acupressure points to help prevent hemorrhaging and then massaged her perineum to encourage the tissues to stretch and allow the head through without tearing.

In birth, as in death, there is no awareness outside that of the present moment. Against the background of having given birth to a baby daughter just eight weeks ago and then of losing her to SIDS, our actions felt grounded in a way that made the intensity of the ordeal seem as ordinary as it was profound. Saima seemed reassured in our presence. Flo and Naomi looked on and provided support while Saima, Melanie and I got on with birthing the baby.

In less than 10 minutes, Karma Sherab Zangpo was born. When his head came out, I recited the mantra of Karmapa to him as I had done for Shamara. I had never assisted at the birth of a baby boy before. He was feisty. I laid him on Saima's belly. Once again I massaged points to prevent bleeding. Saima had not torn. There was minimal blood. She was fine. The baby was fine.

Later that night, in the silence of the cabin, Melanie and I reflected on Sherab Zangpo's birth. What struck us at the time was the similarity of the energy surrounding birth and death. Coming into life. Leaving life. Both are transitions. Entering the Bardo of living in a body - beginning at the moment of birth. And entering the Bardo of consciousness between lives - beginning at the moment of death. We were learning in possibly the most graphic way the truth of what in Buddhism is called the Four Ordinary Foundations: that life is precious; that it is as fragile as a bubble and that one can die at any time; that the lives we experience are the result of our own actions; and that being preoccupied with anything other than spiritual unfoldment is frivolous.

This very personal teaching in the moment also pointed to a larger reality. Ten days earlier we had witnessed the death of Shamara and her rebirth into Amitabha's Pure Land. Miracle after miracle had sharpened our senses. Our trip to Woodstock had felt necessary. At the moment the idea came to us, we were still caught up in the smaller picture of our own need to get away. The larger necessity was that had Melanie and I not been at the monastery 10 days later, we would not have been able to bring Sherab Zangpo into the world. In the bigger picture, there seemed to be a connection between our daughter, named by one of the teachers we venerate the most, and this little boy, born of a Finnish mother and Tibetan father in the lama's house at Karma Triyana Dharmachakra. Perhaps Karma Sherab Zangpo is a reincarnate. Perhaps not. We certainly are not ones to know. But, what we do know and what seems to matter is that Melanie and I were offered events of life and death, of miracles to help us wake up to a vaster, more sacred vision of the world around us. It was our own rebirth into a Pure Land - the Pure Land where all sights, sounds, visions and experiences are none other than expressions of the Buddha.

Of course, there are times where we catch ourselves napping, preoccupied in the mesmerizing web of conditioned three-dimensional reality; what in Buddhism is known as samsara. It is hard to awaken from our habitually reinforced hallucinations. It takes practice. But perhaps what makes it a little easier is when we reflect on the powerful, magical time when the pure practicality of the Dharma - the Buddha's teaching - was made transparently clear in our own lives.

In looking around me, I now see that these opportunities to wake up are always there. Buddha nature is not hiding itself. We just need to uncover our eyes and trust our hearts. Where we are, here and now, is indeed a Pure Land.

CHAPTER NINE

TEN YEARS LATER

S hamara's passing, her rebirth into Dewachen and other transforming events of 10 years past led Melanie and me to make choices in actions and views.

No matter how profound or sacred events may be, they cannot entirely counteract natural - or more accurately, habitual - human instincts and responses. It is not uncommon for couples to be so traumatized by SIDS that their own health deteriorates and they divorce. Returning from Woodstock, Melanie felt empty and purposeless, which led her into a depression. Within a year she was diagnosed with cervical cancer.

I am convinced that the blessing and power of what we experienced gave us the will and strength to face each other and for Melanie to choose life rather than death.

Melanie's direction in life and health was transformed in her meeting of Dr. Vasant Lad while we helped to run the kitchen at the Omega Institute in Rhinebeck, New York. His spirit and the precision and gentleness of Ayurvedic medicine touched her deeply. Within a year, through applying all of what we knew of health care, following Dr. Lad's instructions and cutting through her negative emotional patterns using meditation and self examination, she was free of cancer.

She then decided to begin a correspondence course with Dr. Lad through his Ayurvedic Institute in Albuquerque, New Mexico. Seven years later, after completing the correspondence course, a year-long program with Dr. Lad and applying what she has studied in this discipline and the whole gamut of alternative health care practices we have made it our business to learn, Melanie has published *Ayurvedic Beauty Care*, the consummate modern text on beauty care in Ayurveda.

As for myself, when we returned to Lexington after our trip to Woodstock, I decided that I wanted further training and education and thus pursued a Masters in Social Work. It seemed the most effective means for me to be able to reach more people. I still pursued all of what Melanie and I had been learning in preventive health care. In these times, our friend Rex Lassalle stands out as an inspiration. Seeing more potential in both Melanie and me than we saw in ourselves, Rex prodded and even financed us so that we could explore new directions and find new avenues into the greater alternative and spiritual communities in America and Europe. It is through his kindness that I became inspired to publish a book on Nine-Star Ki Astrology (called *The Complete Guide To Nine-Star Ki*) and study Tibetan Tai Chi. It was he who enabled both Melanie and me to receive all of the Kagyu empowerments at the Kagyu Ngadzo in Denmark in 1989. Possibly because he had faced death himself, Rex was there for us in a time when what we had learned needed to be transformed into practical skills for living - and making a living. He is healer par excellence. We love him dearly and thank him for being there for us.

Seven years after Shamara's passing, Melanie and I gave birth to our son, Jabeth David-Francis. In Tibetan he is called Karma Jigme Dorje. It is ironic that he is most afraid of thunder when his name means "fearless thunderbolt." It is a name given to him by Khenpo Rinpoche who could see Jabeth before he was born. We do not know what his karma is, but he is a blessing to us. In his birth, confidence in the physical level of her being has returned to Melanie. And for Kai and Tina, the light that went out of their eyes seven years earlier returned. They love and dearly care for their little brother in a way that lets us know that they, too, in their short lives also understand about precious human birth and impermanence.

Throughout the years, Khenpo Rinpoche has remained our spiritual father and a third grandfather to our children. In formal practice and helping us in practical living circumstances, he has manifested to us all the actions of a Bodhisattva. As teacher and protector he is - in our eyes - impeccable and beyond reproach. We pray that, until Enlightenment, we travel through time and space with him.

Also, there is our good friend and lama, Ole who, year after year, has stayed with us, bringing one band of Northern Europeans after another to our home for mini-encampments. Ole is a jewel. He is also a revolutionary and rogue - no doubt attributable to his Viking heritage. I am honored to say that I have known him possibly longer than anyone in America. For over 18 years I have studied with him, practiced with him, ridden through various storms of accusations about his teaching methods and behavior. In all of this I see an example of a solid practitioner, totally committed to His Holiness Karmapa and willing to carry out His Holiness' command in as skillful a way as he can - even if that way challenges established lines of authority or policy. I remember the first time I received a blessing from His Holiness. To this day, I feel that same energy with Ole.

I write these final words in a time when there is political unrest in the Kagyu Buddhist community. I am one of those students who has samaya and a strong connection to teachers on opposing sides of the issues being addressed.

After conversations with many Tibetans, lay and religious, monks, lamas and Rinpoches, from the Kagyu and other lineages I fear that westerners are getting caught up in secular Tibetan turf battles. What we are witnessing is not Dharma. It is Tibetan feudal aristocratic politics struggling within itself as it faces exile and, simultaneously, has to deal with modernity and western democratic ideals. It is this package that brought the Dharma to us. We must honor this appropriately, yet at the same time be brave enough to unwrap the package, embrace what it has brought us and let go of the wrappings.

I say this because it is the Dharma taught by Khenpo Rinpoche, Shamar Rinpoche and Ole that made possible our Shamara's Rebirth into Pure Land and our own transformations. This is what we need to take, study and absorb from such teachers. If we allow sectarian or political bias to interfere with taking the true flower of what they are about and what they offer, then the flower will surely die.

In the Buddhist practice known as Seven Points of Mind Training, we are reminded that we can never write anyone off. From the point of sacred outlook, everyone, everything is our teacher. Everything radiates Buddha nature. Teachers and teaching abound. Again, all are reminders that the Pure Land is always here, always now.

To awaken to and become committed to this vision until we truly embrace the world in this way is the only goal worth striving for.

To do so or not to do so is in our hands. It is up to us.

Medicine Buddha Day
October 22, 1993

POSTSCRIPT
AUSPICIOUS COINCIDENCES

As I documented the 10 days and then 10 years of miracles, awakenings and transformations my whole family has undergone in the birth, death and rebirth of Shamara, I could feel a healing happening through the writing. At the same time, although we have come to be more conscious of the interplay between what is and is not seen, I did not anticipate how current events would, once again, reveal the power of those times in another series of auspicious coincidences. Three incidents stand out.

❖ ❖ ❖

On the day after the completion of this manuscript, after teaching a class on the meditation of Medicine Buddha, a friend and participant in the class told me about a job being offered at a local hospice. I thanked her and dismissed it is an unlikely position for me to be accepted in. However, when Monday came, friend Bonnie called again. After interviewing for the job herself, she got the impression that I was an excellent candidate for the position. This call was to again encourage me to interview for the job. So, I called.

I was immediately offered an interview which was to take place within 45 minutes of the call. I was invited for a second interview on Wednesday. I was offered the job on Friday - one week after completing *Rebirth into Pure Land.*

Perhaps it was because I was not looking for a job that this one came to me so easily. Then again, perhaps it was because after 10 years of reflecting on birth, sickness, old age and death and the miracles forever arising before us that I was ready for the opportunity to serve others as we had been served by friends and teachers in the birth, death and rebirth of Shamara.

This latter perspective seems to fit where I see myself these days. It is such an honor and blessing to be able to be present for people in a time when they are mustering all of what they have learned in their entire lives to face what is an unavoidable truth for each one of us. I pray that what has been given to me throughout these times, I can return to others for their benefit. May we all be reborn into a Pure Land!

*T*wo months after starting with Hospice, I was still busy in the evenings, typing the remainder of this text into my word processor. Our friend, Nancy Reinstein, had done as much as she could and it seemed like the remainder of this leg of the journey was to be mine.

I finished typing the manuscript in at 11:30 at night. The house was quiet, save for the hum of the computer. Since the time when I began to build the shrine room in Kentucky for Khenpo Karthar Rinpoche's visit, I had grown accustomed to late nights like this. And, in this familiar atmosphere which has become a sacred time for me, the phone rang. It is unusual for us to get phone calls so late. But, somehow, within the context of my mood and the manuscript's completion, it did not seem strange at all for someone to be calling.

That is possibly why, when I answered the phone, the caller's voice sounded so familiar, so ordinary. It was Laurel, a friend of ours from Kentucky whom I had not spoken with for nearly eight years. She was the friend who, in desperate times for her, would come to visit at 11:30 at night to sit in the nearly-built shrine room or clean our kitchen and leave before we would awaken. For whatever reasons, she needed to be with me and Melanie then. And now, she just wanted to touch base; to fill us in on the details of what her life had become over the last 8 years. There was nothing dramatic or earth-shattering. She just wanted to chat.

We talked for some time as we had done in the past. However, upon hanging up I was struck by my mood, the atmosphere and the fact that somehow, in the writing of this story, I was reconnecting with the energy of that time and being - once again - shown how those events had created such a powerful and time-proof bond with those whose lives we intermingled with then. This message has been confirmed again and again in recent days when talking with Noni Rhodes, our midwife, and other Lexington friends.

Sometimes one doesn't recognize how close one is to another until tragic circumstances arise. This is indeed the case in our relationship with Virginia.

I had met Virginia in 1989 while teaching a shiatsu program in Europe. Melanie met her at the same time and we all decided that in the future we would correspond and that Virginia would try to create opportunities for us to teach in her part of the country. Indeed, Virginia is an excellent organizer and I did stay in her house and teach programs in Tibetan preventive health care practices and astrology over the next few years.

In early 1992, a new lover entered Virginia's life and she became pregnant. They seemed to be well matched and she was very happy to be pregnant. Melanie encouraged her to contact some friends who could provide her with Ayurvedic herbs for use during pregnancy. Being fit and taking all of these herbs (which in the past Melanie had taken and seen great benefits), the pregnancy went well and all indications were that Virginia would give birth to a strong, healthy child in January.

We didn't hear from her for months and then, in January of 1993, her lover called us. His tone of voice was somber and I knew immediately that something was wrong. Just days before her due date, the baby's heart had stopped. Virginia gave birth to a still-born male child. I spoke with her lover at length. Virginia did not want to speak with anyone and both Melanie and I, knowing the space she was in, respected her right to remain out of touch for a while.

Looking back, I see how we were connected to Virginia in this tragedy. I work with an astrological system which operates on 9-year cycles. In this system we each get the opportunity to see how well we have addressed issues from our past in cycles of time which create an environmental and energetic reproduction in which we can examine ourselves. Here Melanie and I were, almost 9 years since Shamara's passing in January of 1984, trying to support Virginia in her loss.

But at that time, the significance of this coincidence escaped me and our relationship with Virginia and her lover became distant and, at times, unpleasant. It was in August of 1993 that I decided to make one last attempt to turn our relationship in a more positive direction. I wrote to Virginia and mailed the letter, trying to give up any expectation that she might respond. It was in this same time period that I decided to write *Rebirth Into Pure Land*.

Virginia never responded to the letter. Melanie and I accepted her choice, but often wondered how she was doing. That is why, over the Memorial Day weekend of 1994, I decided to make contact after nearly a year of awkward silence. Melanie and I felt that with the passing of time, it might now be worth a try.

I called. No one was home. I left a message on her answering machine. That night, Virginia called back. And the conversation which took place was both a profound and surreal reminder of our connection.

At the time I mailed my letter to her and began writing this narrative, Virginia's relationship with her lover was coming to an end. She needed time and space to herself to heal from the loss - as did he. The next several months led to a gradual transformation of what she conceived her life direction and work to be, something both Melanie and I had gone through after Shamara's passing. What is most remarkable in this transformation is where Virginia ended up as a result of her search. On November 15, 1993, Virginia began to work for a local hospice. That was the very day that I began my work with hospice.

During the conversation, neither Virginia nor I wanted to explore how remarkable this sequence of events with all of its parallels and coincidences was. Both of us were in the "how interesting" phase of responding - where one neither wants to be carried away by nor denigrate the obvious invisible forces at work.

As we could not have orchestrated such events to so perfectly demonstrate our connection, it seems just fine to acknowledge and honor that connection and to move on.

❖ ❖ ❖

Enlightened Ones teach us that everything is perfect in the moment. Why is it so hard to believe that the moments they speak of are no different than the ones we live in here and now?

A LETTER AND EPILOGUE FROM MIDWIFE NONI RHODES

Dear Melanie and Bob,

Here, finally, is the result of your simple request. I do not know why this was such a difficult task for me to perform. With all good intentions I have written and rewritten this account many times. It is not perfect, but I know that it is time to turn it loose.

...My family asks me to say hello. Kelly [Noni's daughter - ed.] is writing her own account of Shamara. I have encouraged her (so what took **me** so long?) to write this and send it to Kai.

Writing about Shamara and reading your account has been healing for me. I still find unbidden tears as I sit down to this task.

We love you all.

Noni

Noni's Epilogue

Shamara was born softly, gently and welcomed in joyous ceremony by her family and friends. I was a privileged witness to the beauty and vitality of her tiny being. That Shamara would pass as softly and swiftly as morning showers did not occur to me. In my mind's eye I see her wise countenance peering out of her mother's warm coat, papoosed carefully into her infant "front pack." I smiled to see the mother and proud big sisters stroll our neighborhood on daily outings. She was cherished.

The effect of Shamara's passing was profound. Shock, grief, sadness, anger, bewilderment name but do not express the tumultuous emotion which grips body and soul like a storm surfacing and resurfacing unbidden. Kai was best friends with my daughter, Kelly. I remember them talking and retelling the story of Shamara. Then the story stopped and silence took its place. Their play was punctuated by strong words of anger, unaccountably.

Making meaning from loss is the healing energy which propels us forward. It does not appear instantaneously, but evolves beginning with love (birth), loss of love (death - or so we feel at the time) resulting in anger, sadness and grief. Only in experiencing these can we move forward to meaning, greater strength and understanding. It is then that we say, "I was privileged to know this remarkable soul."

❖ ❖ ❖

GLOSSARY

Avalokitesvara *(ah-vah-lo-kee-tesh-vah-ra)* - Sanskrit name for the Bodhisattva of Compassion who was originally one of the main disciples of the Buddha. In Tibetan he is called Chenrezig.

Bodhisattva *(bo-dhee-saht-vah)* - an adept of the Mahayana path who can no longer fall into the confusion of mundane reality (samsara) and is committed to the liberation of all beings caught in such.

Chenrezig *(chehn-ray-zig)* - the Tibetan name for the Bodhisattva of Compassion. His mantra is OM MANI PEME HUNG (Ohm-mah-nee-peh-meh-hoong) [Tibetan].

Damaru *(dah-mah-ru)* a hand-held, double-sided drum used in certain Buddhist practices.

Dewachen *(deh-wah-chen)* - the "pure land" of the Amitah-ba Buddha, the Buddha of Discriminating Awareness. It is also called the Western Pure Land and is the easiest of the pure lands to be reborn into from our plane of existence.

Dharma *(dahr-mah)* - the truth or "way things are" as

taught by the Buddha. There are worldly dharmas or relative truths and ultimate dharma, which is what the Buddha taught about the nature of reality.

Dharmadhatu *(dahr-mah-dah-too)* - in this context, one of the local centers under the umbrella of Vajradhatu, the organization set up under the guidance of the Vajracarya Chogyam Trungpa Rinpoche.

Four Noble Truths - the first teaching of the Buddha after His enlightenment. Essentially, these four truths are that regardless of whether or not we see it clearly, life based on anything but the truth of how reality actually is, is suffering; that the cause of this suffering is our ego clinging to our misperceptions of reality; that there is a way out of this suffering; and that way is the Middle Way, or learning how to see things as they truly are and to act and live in accordance with that truth.

Kagyu *(kah-gyoo)* - one of the four main lineages of Tibetan Buddhism. It is also called the Practice Lineage or Mishap Lineage. Its main teacher is His Holiness the Gyalwa Karmapa.

Kagyu Samye *(sam-yeh)* **Ling** - one of the first and foremost meditation centers in the West, located in Eskdalemuir, Scotland. Originally started by Ven. Chogyam Trungpa Rinpoche and Akong Rinpoche.

Kalu *(kah-loo)* **Rinpoche** - one of the great yogis of the Kagyu Lineage. It is currently a young boy training at his own monastery in Sonada, India.

Karma *(kahr-mah)* - the law of cause and effect. It is what we experience from our actions. However, it does not imply that everything is predestined. We affect our future karma by how we respond to the circumstances and situations we find ourselves in as a result of our previous actions. Thus, although we cannot change the past, how we deal with the present will have a direct effect on what we will experience in the future.

Karmapa *(kahr-mah-pah)* - also called Gyalwa Karmapa. Karmapa means "he who performs the activity of a Buddha" or, briefly, Man of Action. He is the main teacher and center of the Kagyu Lineage, the first of the reincarnates of Tibet to return as the same being lifetime after lifetime. He is called the Knower of the Three Times, because his energy, power and awareness make him beyond time and capable of seeing into and acting on behalf of sentient beings in all places and times. He is currently in his 17th incarnation. His sacred mantra or chant is KARMAPA CHENO (Kahr-mah-pah Chay-noh).

Karma Triyana Dharmachakra - The main seat of His Holiness the Gyalwa Karmapa, located in Woodstock, New York.

Khenpo Karthar Rinpoche *(ken-poh kahr-tahr)* - abbot of Karma Triyana Dharmachakra, the seat of His Holiness the Gyalwa Karmapa in America. Khenpo means abbot and Karthar is an abbreviation of his full name, Karma Tharchen. He is regarded as one of the finest Dharma masters in the West and is respected by all lineages for his vast knowledge of the vehicles and commentaries of Buddhism.

Lama *(lah-ma)*- a person who is recognized for his/her meditative accomplishment and is bestowed with this title as a distinction and also as an acknowledgement of the ability to teach others.

Lama Ole Nydahl - One of the first western students, along with his wife, Hannah, of His Holiness the 16th Gyalwa Karmapa. His Holiness directed Ole and Hannah to many teachers in Asia and then entrusted Ole to teach throughout Europe and begin the process of opening up centers in America and around the world. His teacher is Tenga Rinpoche who has directed Ole to teach Phowa or the conscious dying practice of Tibetan Buddhism to as many students as possible. He now acts under the direction of the Ven. Shamar Rinpoche.

Mikyo Dorje *(mih-kyoh dohr-jay)* - the 8th historical Gyalwa Karmapa.

Ngodrup Burkhar *(noo-droop boor-kar)* - one of the foremost translators for Kagyu teachers in America and Asia.

Phowa *(poh-wah)* - the special meditative practice that is for the transference of consciousness at the time of dying. The transference that is focused on is where the being's consciousness leaves the body from the crown of the head and enters into Dewachen, the Pure Land of the Amitabha Buddha.

Pure Land - a celestial realm which is a manifestation of and presided over by an enlightened being. Beings reborn into a pure land are given the opportunity to do spiritual practice without distraction and with the blessing of whichever enlightened being's pure land it is.

Refuge - a formal ceremony one undergoes to be considered an official member of the Buddhist community. One is taking "refuge" in beings who exemplify our enlightened potential, their teachings (Dharma) and the community which practices in accordance with these teachings.

Rinpoche *(rihn-poh-shay)* - means Precious One, usually an incarnate or "tulku" who has consciously returned to a realm of relative beings to teach the Dharma and help them to reach enlightenment.

Samaya *(sah-mai-yah)* - a sacred bond of commitment to a teacher and the teachings he or she gives.

Sangha *(sahn-gah)* - the community of those who practice and study the teachings of the Buddha.

Sharmapa *(shahr-mah-pah)* - also called His Eminence Shamar Rinpoche. Shamar Rinpoche is one of the Four Regents of the Kagyu Lineage. He is an emanation of the Amitabha Buddha and has reincarnated throughout time along with His Holiness the Gyalwa Karmapa. He is currently in his 13th incarnation.

Stupa - a three dimensional symbolic representation of the path to enlightenment and enlightenment itself. The historical Buddha was supposedly to have seen this form in space.

USEFUL ADDRESSES

To learn more about the teachings and schedule of Ven.
Khenpo Karthar Rinpoche, contact:
> Karma Triyana Dharmachakra
> 352 Meads Mountain Road
> Woodstock, NY 12498
> (914)679-5906

To learn more about the teachings of Ole Nydahl and his
courses on Phowa, contact:

> Karma Jigme Ling
> 33 Marne Avenue
> San Francisco, CA 94127
> (415)661-6467

> or

> Karma Drub Djy Ling
> Svanemollevej 56
> 2100 Copenhagen
> DENMARK

For information about SIDS (Sudden Infant Death Syndrome), contact:

National SIDS Alliance
10500 Little Patuxent Pkwy. Suite 420
Columbia, MD 21044
(800)221-7437

For information about local hospice services, contact:

National Hospice Organization
1901 North Moore St. Suite 901
Arlington, VA 22209
(800)646-6460

To contact the author and his family, write to:

Bob and Melanie Sachs
Robertsachs2020@gmail.com
Tel: 805-904-6408

May all beings benefit.

May we all realize the Pure Land.

Other books by Zivah Publishers

Sedona - Sacred Earth by Nicholas R. Mann

This book looks at the spectacular landmarks of Arizona's Red Rock Country and suggests some startling interpretations. By the application of concepts drawn from geomancy and from the examination of the Native American myths, a pattern of sacred sites and geometrical and animal figures emerges from the Sedona landscape.
100 pp - Softcover - $10.95 - ISBN 0-9622707-3-3.

Pathways to Your Three Selves by Wayne A. Guthrie, D.D. and Bella Karish, D.D.

This is the Wisdom of YOUR Three Selves! Brought forth to assist you in understanding and integrating your Three Levels of Consciousness. It can help you to live a more balanced and harmonious life.
107 pp - Softcover - $8.95 - ISBN 0-9622707-1-7

In Harmony - Resolving Stress by Marcia Sutton, Ph.D.

This book's purpose is to help you make changes in yourself, in your lifestyle and habits, in your surroundings, in anything that is causing you stress. 306 pp - Softcover 8½ x 11 workbook - $25.95 - ISBN 0-9620500-0-8

Order Form

Zivah Publishers - P.O. Box 13192, Albuquerque, NM 87192-3192

Qty.	Title	Price	Total
		Subtotal	
		Tax (NM only)	
		Shipping - Add 20% of subtotal	
		TOTAL	

Please enclose check or money order for the TOTAL amount. Allow 3-4 weeks for delivery. Don't forget to give us the name and address of where the books are to be sent if different than the name and address on your check. Bookstore discount is available.